ADVANCE AUSTRALIA FAIR

AN ANGUS & ROBERTSON BOOK
An imprint of HarperCollinsPublishers

First published in Australia in 1991
Reprinted in 1991
CollinsAngus&Robertson Publishers Pty Limited (ACN 009 913 517)
A division of HarperCollinsPublishers (Australia) Pty Limited
4 Eden Park, 31 Waterloo Road, North Ryde, NSW 2113, Australia
HarperCollinsPublishers (New Zealand) Limited
31 View Road, Glenfield, Auckland 10, New Zealand
HarperCollinsPublishers Limited
77– 85 Fulham Palace Road, London W6 8JB, United Kingdom

National Library of Australia
Cataloguing-in-Publication data:

McCormick, P. D. (Peter Dodds).
    Advance Australia fair

    ISBN 0 207 17006 1.

National songs – Australia – Texts. I. Title
A782.4215990268

Cover painting : A Breakaway by Tom Roberts (1856–1931)
Oil on canvas 137.2 x 168.1cm
Elder Bequest Fund
Art Gallery of South Australia, Adelaide

Previous page: Still Life with National Flowers by Margaret Preston (1883–1963)
Oil on canvas 50 x 50cm
Gift of the Margaret Preston Estate 1977
Art Gallery of New South Wales

Opposite : An Old Bee Farm by Clara Southern (1861–1940)
Oil on canvas 66 x 111.7cm
Felton Bequest 1942
National Gallery of Victoria

Printed in Australia by Griffin Press

5   4   3   2
95 94 93 92 91

ADVANCE AUSTRALIA FAIR

composed by Peter Dodds McCormick

Angus&Robertson
An imprint of HarperCollins*Publishers*

Australians all let us rejoice,

Dancing Children No. 1 - **Russell Drysdale**

The harsh, empty outback so often depicted in Russell Drysdale's paintings is softened here by joyful children dancing in its boundless space.

Russell Drysdale 1912-1981
Dancing Children No.1
Oil on canvas 30.5 x 40.6 cm
Private Collection

For we are young and free;

Bush Idyll - **Frederick McCubbin**

Soft shadows and colours indicate that Frederick McCubbin saw the bush as a gentle place. 'You only have to wait and watch her varying moods,' he said, 'and you will find all the beauty you can desire.' McCubbin also loved children and believed that they found the bush a place of mystery and enchantment.

Frederick McCubbin 1855-1917
Bush Idyll
Oil on canvas 119.5 x 221.5cm
On loan to the Newcastle Region Art Gallery

We've golden soil and wealth for toil,

A Hot Day - David Davies

The glowing gold and blue in many paintings of the Australian landscape signifies the rich and fertile nature of this land. This painting portrays the glare and heat of a midsummer's day.

David Davies 1864-1939
A Hot Day
Oil on canvas 60.6 x 91.3cm
Felton Bequest 1937
Reproduced by permission of
the National Gallery of Victoria, Melbourne

Our home is girt by sea.

Diamond Bay - John Perceval

This vivid view of the Victorian coastline captures the excitement of the ocean as well as showing the barrier these dangerous waters form between our isolated continent and the rest of the world.

John Perceval 1923-1987
Diamond Bay
Oil on hardback 91 x 122cm
Painted in situ at Sorrento January 1957
Private Collection

Our land abounds in nature's gifts,

Palm Valley - Albert Namatjira

Waterholes and springs bring life to the arid centre of Australia. Palm Valley was Albert Namatjira's dreaming place and he painted it many times.

Albert Namatjira 1902-1959
Palm Valley
Watercolour on paper 37 x 54cm
Purchased 1986
Art Gallery of New South Wales

Of beauty rich and rare;

Summer - **Hans Heysen**

Hans Heysen delighted in drawing and painting the natural world, particularly the gum trees found in and around the ranges of South Australia. He was fascinated with light – with how it slanted through the leaves or fell on the pale trunks and peeling bark of these massive trees.

Hans Heysen 1877-1963
Summer
Watercolour on paper 56.5 x 78.4cm
Purchased 1909
Art Gallery of New South Wales

In history's page, let every stage, Advance Australia Fair.

In joyful strains then let us sing, Advance Australia Fair.

The Opening of the First Parliament of the Commonwealth - Tom Roberts

When Tom Roberts was invited to record the opening ceremony, he was asked to make 'correct representations of the Duke and Duchess of York, the Governor-General, the state governors, members of the Federal Parliament and 250 other distinguished guests.' This took many hours of work, including trips overseas to make sure the portraits were accurate.

Tom Roberts 1856-1931
The Opening of the First Parliament of the Commonwealth
of Australia by HM King George V, 9 May 1901
Oil on canvas 305 x 510cm
Royal collection on permanent loan to
the people of Australia

Beneath our radiant Southern Cross,

Native Flowers of NSW - **Margaret Preston**

The native flowers depicted here beneath the Southern Cross are blue orchids, Christmas bells, the waratah, flannel flowers and banksia.

Margaret Preston 1883-1963
Native Flowers of N.S.W
Colour monotype 38.5 x 36.0cm
Private Collection

We'll toil with hearts and hands;

The Sock Knitter - Grace Cossington-Smith

Grace Cossington-Smith used square brushstrokes of solid colour to capture the life and warmth of this woman knitting socks for the war effort.

Grace Cossington-Smith 1892-1984
The Sock Knitter
Oil on canvas 61.6 x 50.7cm
Purchased 1960
Art Gallery of New South Wales

To make this Commonwealth of ours,

Gippsland, Sunday Night, February 20th, 1898 - John Longstaff

Natural disasters like this bushfire are common and have helped forge the
Australian character.

John Longstaff 1862-1941
Gippsland, Sunday Night, February 20th, 1898
Oil on canvas 196.2 x 143.5cm
Purchased 1898
Reproduced by permission of
the National Gallery of Victoria, Melbourne

Renowned of all the lands.

The Man with the Donkey - Horace Moore-Jones

This painting by the war artist, Horace Moore-Jones, is of Richard Henderson, one of the Australian soldiers at Gallipoli. Like Simpson before him, Henderson undertook the brave task of carrying the wounded from the battlefield down to the beach on a donkey.

Horace Moore-Jones 1868-1922
The Man with the Donkey
Watercolour with pencil 102.6 x 75.3cm
On loan to the Australian War Memorial
from the Australian National Gallery

For those who've come across the seas,

Coming South - Tom Roberts

Tom Roberts did the sketches for this painting on a voyage from England back to Australia. It portrays the crowded deck of a steamer with its cargo of migrants bound for a new life in the brash young cities, new mining towns or the vast outback of Australia.

We've boundless plains to share;

Irrigation Lake, Wimmera - **Arthur Boyd**

Boyd enlivens the traditional blue and gold of the Australian wheatfield landscape with the black figures of crows and the stark white of drowned trees.

With courage let us all combine,
To Advance Australia Fair.

In joyful strains then let us sing,
Advance Australia Fair.

Field Naturalists - Jane Sutherland

Three children, at home in the landscape, capture the spirit of Australia
with their enquiring interest in the natural world.

ADVANCE AUSTRALIA FAIR

	DATE DUE